Skin. Hair. Bones.

poems by

Maria McLeod

Finishing Line Press
Georgetown, Kentucky

Skin. Hair. Bones.

Copyright © 2022 by Maria McLeod
ISBN 978-1-64662-883-4 First Edition
All rights reserved under International and Pan-American Copyright Conventions. No part of this book may be reproduced in any manner whatsoever without written permission from the publisher, except in the case of brief quotations embodied in critical articles and reviews.

ACKNOWLEDGMENTS

Grateful acknowledgment is offered to the editors of the following publications where these works first appeared:

Skin. Hair. Bones.—*Critical Quarterly*
The S of Sin—*Sow's Ear Poetry Review*
Soul to Take—*Harpoon Review*
With This Skin—*Cream City Review*
The Meaning of Marriage—*Quarter After Eight*
The B of Betrayal—*Puerto del Sol*
Fathom—*Up the Staircase Review*
Ghosts of Those—*The Penn Review*
These Bodies—*Noisy Water: Poetry from Whatcom County, Washington*

Publisher: Leah Huete de Maines
Editor: Christen Kincaid
Cover Art and Design: Rowan Moore-Seifred
Author Photo: Stephen S. Howie

Order online: www.finishinglinepress.com
also available on amazon.com

Author inquiries and mail orders:
Finishing Line Press
PO Box 1626
Georgetown, Kentucky 40324
USA

Table of Contents

Skin. Hair. Bones. 1

The S of Sin 2

Soul to Take 4

With This Skin 6

The Meaning of Marriage 9

Guest Room 10

The B of Betrayal 11

Translation 12

The G of Guilt 14

Trapeze 15

Fathom 17

Why I Chose Him 18

Tragedy Unfolding 20

To Sleep Forever 22

Shutter 24

Ghosts of Those 25

These Bodies 26

Skin. Hair. Bones.

This is not a body I can believe in. It is the body I called from the sky. Skin. Hair. Bones. It is a body I brought to myself. A gift. I called to it. Said, *muscle, mouth, cock.* The wrist. The inside of his arm. Soft. It came to me, a boy. Not a boy. A man. Yet, not whole—ephemeral, fragmentary. This skin I touch now is lost to me, to him. He will lose it; it comes off. But there is replication, regeneration. Come. It comes back, returns. Skin to dust, dust to skin. My mouth at his wrist, the tender circles I draw with my tongue; and at the back of his leg, behind his knee. The kiss on the inside of his arm, at the bend. At the top of his neck, under his chin. Where the skin is untouched, vulnerable, smooth, penetrable. To touch between his fingers, his toes, the slick tip of tongue to cock. The ends of his fingers in my mouth, the ends of my fingers in his mouth. To suck. Sacramental. A rite, ritual. To come into and to pass through. The body diaphanous, ethereal. He, a passing shadow beneath me, to the side of me, on top of me, inside. Outside of me: words, breathing, breath. To demarcate, claim our territory. To scratch is to cut, to bite, bruise. Heal, to undo what has been done. Erase. Saliva, semen, spit. My bleeding, an accident decorating his torso, his thighs. That which comes without warning. An indication, an omen. Open, an opening. The eyes. The blue-grey color of the iris. A door we leave through while there are words, last rites, still to speak. But he is see-through, an apparition, illusion. His body thin, delicate. Womanly. His arms spread apart; I grasp his wrists, hold them at his sides to the bed. A crucifixion. *My own sweet Jesus.* My words travel into the air, decompose, diffuse, break apart, collapse. See how he turns and turns.

The S of Sin

S is the body's seal
broken, the escape
of heat, the tease, the fine lace of air passing
between the lips, winding its way
through teeth, taking over tongue as the orbits
of our mouths are liberated from the work
of words. S, so skilled, carves out the body's fate,
biblical and tortured, and teaches us
to eat of it, teaches us
to take.

The *I*
is the fruit
of the word,
the stone
swallowed, taking us
to an unlit underworld,
a cave of blind insects.
We are
without eyes
in the Earth's belly,
reduced to touch and taste
and smell. Sour stench
of magma, slick sheath of skin.
We lose sense
of one body's beginning
and the other's end.
Volcanic this bed
of heat, how badly
we need
to drink.

N, embedded in the throat
of the word, leaks up
from underground.
We heard it as children, ears to the earth,
thunder of floods our parents never predicted.
Yet, the N of sin is not an end, but that low moan
entering the spidery bones of the feet, climbing
the solid staffs of leg, the pelvis and its winged hips,
traveling the monkey tails of our spines,
fiery path of nerve and synapse,
relentless spin of cells
in the bones of the face.
Shamed and pleasured, we name it
drowning, yet we live, breathing out, drinking it in.

Soul to Take

She is come hither horrific:
form of the plague, form in the grass,
thistle, nettle, widow's lace

pressed between pages, words
cast afloat like boats
without oars.

*Now I lay me
down to sleep.*

The stench of her sex —
eyelet, slit—where, O
of her mouth, she disappears you.
cavern, well.

*I pray the lord
my soul to keep.*

her lips pressed
to the curve of your chest, a prayer
you recite for lack
of air.

should I die before I wake,

She traces the baby bones
at the base of your throat.
Night breaks
over her back; your world
goes black.

*I pray the lord my soul
to take.*

You're emptied
into an unlit hollow:
knotweed, pigwort, chokecherry.
Say her name. Spit it out.

With This Skin

Once, I was as clean
as a new sheet stretched tight and tucked in
at all four corners, on my way
to a place good girls don't go.
I met a sweet, strung-out boy man,
guitar in his hands, some muscle.
I won't lie: I was your run-of-the-mill
missionary. I didn't want to waste myself,
but give him something else to thirst for.
Like a bartender lining up shots,
I put myself on the countertop.

July 1982:
*I have gone to jail tonight to pay them to release my lover,
because my lover, drunk, tried to kill a man. Drunk and stoned or
hallucinating, he had run over a man, but missed his body and only
hit his leg and the man fell down in the night and someone thought
they heard a deep, deep moan but all were sure they had seen him
fall backward in that eternal fall backward that happens in slow
motion. And someone said the man's body twitched for a moment
after the car drove too fast and right at the man who didn't have
time to run but looked up to see the face of a driver already afraid
of what he had done.*

When we met, I was a waitress,
he, part fry cook, part musician.
On that first day, he clutched his spatula
to his chest, followed me
with his eyes. His baby-blue t-shirt, torn
at the shoulder. Long hair, a greasy, matted mess.
It took him two weeks
to speak.

Revival became my one great talent.
I offered something better
than another all-night drunk.
He was my pet
project, my home away from hell
where I grew up. He was my baby,
my big man, more
than I bargained for.

November 1983:
There are days when I'm small, when I am the girl, when his hand is too large and his arm is too strong. Days when my mind fades out too soon, then not soon enough, when my lover drinks too much and he finds me seeing myself in his mirror, my face is too much in his house and he cannot stand it there. I'm pushed into that face, cut, shattered. I leave myself, walk and walk away, down the street, not in my body but removed and waiting for my lover to come back.

This story is no different
than those told about the momentary dead,
spirits hovering over their own dying bodies,
hearts stopped at the accident scene,
drifting between their former worldly existence
and the afterlife.

I float above the clinking glasses,
seeing us, two young lovers just off work,
trying to make it in the dark
back booth, skirt bunched around my waist.
We have onlookers,
but I'm too delirious with this skin
I'm shedding. I don't look back, but I do
look forward, seduced by the body I see
reflected in the eyes I'm facing.

July 1982:
It's dark and he didn't mean to do it. Make out the words, hit and run, man run over. Words of the mouth: pathetic, half human, why don't I die, why not dead. The sounds slide one after another, slur, collapse, run out. There are tears and, sorry, I'm so sorry. I soothe him, smooth his hair. This is the before and after: the anger behind the headlights followed by the fear of the body fallen backward. Collision of two moments, hit and run.

When she hits the mirror,
and all that glass spills forward,
I recognize the sound of dimes
hitting the pavement.
She's already outside
herself.
My impulse is to thrust my arm out,
protect that person I was from walking
into traffic. But I'm here, alone

and suspended in retrospect.
When he rises and opens
his arms to greet me,
it is the last place I want to remember
having crawled into.

The Meaning of Marriage

We agree to meet at the faux Victorian, the addition you're building to resemble the existing house, which, like the marriage of its owners, is falling apart. Still, you follow their design, frame the walls, raise a roof so steeply pitched you can't climb onto it without tethering yourself to the scaffolding. It's the end of your day; your crew's gone. You lead me up the unfinished staircase, hand grazing the middle of my back, and guide me into the master bedroom they'll never sleep in together. You take me to the spot the bed will occupy and point out the twin rectangles you've cut into the sheathing, future skylights giving way to the blue I'm soon to enter.

When we were young, we'd take shelter in half-built houses like this, and I'd trace your needle tracks. Now I walk the perimeter, remind myself of the meaning of marriage. In a few hours, I'll take flight, cross the country, and be home before the scent of sawdust leaves my hair. Here, we're open to the elements, standing quietly on opposite sides of see-through walls. In the pause we bump into, I notice your knees are tender, red from a day spent working the roof. I want to rub my palms across them, smooth out the shingle marks. You point out the inadequate dimensions. It's too small, you say, explaining that the bedroom you and your wife share is surely bigger. You ask about my husband, and I say, truthfully, *he misses me.*

We're standing still between the studs, holding ourselves apart. We don't know the fate of the owners, their children, which rooms they'll inhabit, who will stay and who will go. My fingers find a knot in a two-by-four. I circle the shape of it. The kiln-dried wood smells warm, smells real, but its exposure is temporary. Like every board you've nailed up, it's soon to disappear under sheetrock. No one can know what, years from now, might bleed through and what will seem to have never existed.

Guest room

She wakes to lipstick stains
on the pillowcase and a bottle of spilled pills
scattered across someone else's nightstand,
confused to find herself, limbs spread
in a tabloid pose, scene of the starlet's suicide,
caption reading: "victim was nude."

Her clothes, strewn across the room,
incite recollection: she had arrived
too late, too drunk. She had let him
undress her. What then? Sounds seep through
the walls: a child, a dog, breakfast
in the making. *Guest room.* She remembers
his wife saying it, asking him to show her to it.

It is February, the month when the world
stands still, when nothing
worth talking about happens.
She drops aspirin—the pills
— back into their bottle. *Nothing,*
she says aloud, finding her mouth
dry, lips chapped. She collects her clothes
from the floor, strips the bed, disappears
her imprint from the sheet.

The B of Betrayal

The *B* of betrayal is the bed of the river
where she backstrokes, head
half sunk, body half afloat,
blessed by sky, oblivious
to the earth beneath her
where cedar and tamarack turn water
copper and walleyes rise
to inspect her back.

Keeping to the current,
she comes upon the twist, the shift
in light, a bend—breach
of trust. Here, escaped bait
embed themselves in silt
while eddies churn icy at her heels.

They meet once a week; she
and her lover lower the shades
and pray their simple spouses trust them.

She wrestles the river, jaw square, teeth clenched,
but then gives way. *Betray.* She lets the word anchor, float
in her mouth, lay the tongue flat, complicit
with the source of sound, a break wall in the heart
of her throat. *Betrayal.* In this she participates, swims
as if all she knows is the continuous slice
of surface against her hands, left
then right, eyes to sky,
waits for her feet

to touch, for the back of her head to hit
something solid enough to wake her.

Translation

As you kissed her, 2:27 a.m., I woke
to find my pillowcase wet with spit
and snot. My room was closed up, airless.
The bed, hollowed out
like an old, wooden canoe I'd sunk
into. It was a slow moment
of recognition, a sixth sense
that woke me, breathing heaved, uneven.

Some blocks away, your car's dash
cast an easy green glow
in the half-lit night. I rose
to wash my face
as she was asking you to climb the stairs
to her apartment, to stay.

You wanted to so, the allure
of her accent, the evening
you'd spent dancing, irresistible, all
she didn't know of us.

I found myself in the mirror, red,
a face I couldn't place, emotion unattached
to memory, like something foul
I had accidentally swallowed —
your desire to disappear
in another—the known unknown
I'd tried to purge in my sleep.

While I brought water to my face, you looked
toward your hands and said, *I can't.*
She shook her head, and, in a foreign tongue
said (of me), *Elle est chiante.* You could not
translate, but assumed she cursed you for a night
wasted. Instead, it was your curse
that entered your head.

You left for your own bed
and a fitful sleep, a nightmare
on repeat: my body roped
to the ceiling above you, feet swaying
in your face, and your inability to wake
and rid yourself of me.
Each annoyed attempt to bat me away
bringing on the return: my two terrible feet
at your face.

The G of Guilt

The *G* of guilt is the eyes
of the word, spying misdeeds
relived in our heads, the root
of restless sleep. *G* sees
into our animal hearts, locates the bone,
the crooked stick.
The vowels follow, the *UI*
an illness, an ulcer, an acidic
curse we keep like a scar
etched into our skin. How instinctive
guilt; so like a dog
crouched, tail tucked,
eyes lowered, then lifted
slightly—her admission—as she passed over
the scene of her crime. Likewise
the *L* of guilt licks
the ground, lingering as sound held
in the mouth, inhabiting
with a weight like grief.
T, the spear of truth,
pierces the skin, a wound
reminding us we are mortal.
Our tongues to our teeth,
we end like this, carnivorous,
regretting the flesh
we've dared to eat.

Trapeze

We were two of a kind, wearing black
and scratching scars
into our arms. We couldn't wait
for the scabs to fall away, to read
our self-inflicted injuries, our own names
etched in each other's flesh.
Seventeen and already in love
with misery, we fit together like fork
and knife. If I close my eyes
I can see our reflection, our bodies joined
in the broken mirrors circling our secluded spot
in the vacant lot.

On our first date, I admitted I was in love
with the trapeze, all those wild leaps
of faith like so many kisses
with death. So he took me
to the circus where we slugged
whiskey beneath the bleachers, below
the happy families. Where they roared
over the elephants, we were transfixed
by the sequined woman: the one who spun
by her thick black hair from the end
of a rope—her face a whirling blur, her legs splayed
in a mid-air splits. To watch her made us dizzy
with a guilty pleasure. When she finally came
to a stop, one could see she wore the plastered smile
of beauty queens. Amidst applause, I noticed she was bleeding
from her scalp. A thick rivulet
trickled down her porcelain face
like the beginning
of a fracture.

I can't remember if that was the first night
we spent together; I can only recall
that we fought on the way back to the car.
Wanting to wait out the effects of the flask,
I tossed the keys into a dumpster,
but he hoisted me up and over
that metal lip, into the stench. I bit
the inside of my cheeks
to keep from calling to him, to show him
I could take what he dished out.
It was as if I thought love was borne
of a tolerance to pain. I wanted him
to ruin me, and in ruining me,
make me whole.

Fathom

when finally we went lip to lip our hips
hinged our knees knocked our hairs
singed to salt blown into the face
of the sun as it spun out of the sky
doors sealed shut and shutters
slapped together like mad wives
and curtains swished closed as coats
midwinter under snow and stars
blinking out as we buried our former loves
a fathom beneath the muck
we became what the earth coughed up
we were dirt we were ash we were children
raised by wolves we were filth
we were chewed off at the ankles the wrists
we were out of the trap we were so alive
we were the blood of birth we were bone
marrying bone we were without ceremony
or ceiling or floor or clock we
were spit starved broken divinely
open we dined on each other
we were so ripe we went rotten

Why I Chose Him

I chose him not because he was kind
or handsome or selfless.
I chose him because he promised
he wouldn't leave me
maimed or misaligned
or deformed.
It was his arrogance that wooed me,
his brash self-assuredness.
I had let him feel the bullet
in my breast, the still growing
tumor I needed to be rid of.
He had used that sacred word,
cure. He said he could cure me.
He had paused after he said it,
blinking, looking right at me,
waiting, perhaps thinking,
This is the line she'll bite on;
this is the line
that will seal the deal.
It was the end of his day.
He looked like he wanted
to undo his tie, to go home,
to pour himself a brandy
and sit by the fire, pondering
his God-like status.
But, first, he needed me
to decide, to agree
to the treatment
he was proposing.

I asked if my afflicted breast
would be made smaller, disfigured,
my nipple lifted off
and reattached. I considered
the horrors of what
I'd have to contend
with, my once-perfect breast
sliced and diced, a small
compromise so that
I may live. I remember
wanting to sound educated,
unintimidated, fearless
in confronting it, but he was so full
of himself, his medical magnificence
filled the room, and I couldn't help
but feel small in the face of it.
I was but one more
patient who needed him
to assure her of his ability
to cut her open, to remove
what would otherwise
kill her and then to stitch her up.
The truth is, I didn't like him
at all. Of course, he was lying
about the fine condition
he'd leave me in. He'd made
an empty promise.
I'd live, but my breast
would never again
look like my breast, not after
I'd let him cut into me, not after
I'd said yes.

Tragedy, unfolding

The ceiling fan circles; my bedroom
cooks. In the city, such heat

drives damage. Already
I've ground my eyeteeth flat.

Downstairs, the neighbor kid
goes berserk, slits

his drug dealer's throat. Straight
razor. He takes off, tripping

on the cuffs of his phat pants, falls.
If I listen for it,

I can hear the toilet run, the sink
drip. An ambulance driver

waits for what's next.
If only I could trust

these teeth will remain apart
while I sleep. Nights like this

I lie naked—no blanket, no sheet,
like the filmic version

of the innocent who remains unaware
tragedy is unfolding, that she

could be next.
The kid gets up, keeps running.

As sirens slice through ribbons
of heat, I can't help

but clench my teeth.
We all die

how we live,
without relief.

To Sleep Forever

It wasn't that I wanted to sleep forever,
but rather, I didn't want to wake
to my missing parts making their way
to a far-off medical lab
where I imagine my ovaries and uterus
and tangle of Fallopian tubes
spilling over their Petri dishes,
awaiting dissection, determinants
of my fate.

Not quite a sleeping beauty,
my face had grown fat
from the fluids it collected
while my body was inverted
on the angled operating table,
head dipped toward the floor,
legs raised, feet in stirrups,
surgeon between my knees
working on the laborious excavation.

All these years, those organs
had cursed me. *Socked in*
is how my surgeon described
my atrophied lady parts adhered
to the cavity just above my sacrum,
requiring her to dig and snip and slice
in order to pluck them out.

Of course, I didn't want to wake
from such a lovely stupor, my bliss
of unknowing. Who among us
wants to witness the atrocities
of her own body's failings?
Even with my loved ones waiting
and wondering if I'd ever wake
from my anesthesia-induced coma,
I chose to wallow in the netherworld
with its gift of amnesia, seduced
by my own absence.

What better way to stave off sorrow
than to luxuriate in the abyss
of pitch-black sleep, to cradle myself
in a temporary shelter
grief can't reach?

Shutter

History unrecorded, we dwell
in the collective unconscious, ephemera
cast afloat. We appear
in black & white, squatters
in a film played in a smoky room
where we rise up in a single shaft of light.
The fragile footage dissolves
under the heat of the projector's lamp.
Even the faintest outline of us burns up.

The Ghosts of Those

Our legs dangle over the edge of this Detroit
rooftop. The eight-story Uniroyal tire,
a clearly visible sentry, presides over East I-94.
Below us foreign cars, once hated entities, stop and start
at the intersection of a Domino's Pizza
and a 24-hour party store, still selling
Stroh's Dark and Zig-Zags as if it were perpetually 1974.
We are would-be lovers. Like would-be assassins,
or would-be rock stars, we've become good
at dressing the part, but display no skill
in creating convincing characters.
We hold hands and whisper, *I can't
resist you*, even though we can and do resist.
Instead we drink straight from our shared bottle, blow kisses
at traffic lights, and toast our steadfast spouses
who know us too well to suspect the worst.
The truth is evident, if only to us: the giant tire
was once a Ferris wheel until it was encased
in rubber, forever entombing the swinging seats.
It holds the ghosts of those who left the fairgrounds
for the treetops, sweetly kissing the curve of the horizon,
their world below rendered miniature.
Even now, we take joy in remembering
the expectant, upturned faces of those in line,
standing where we once stood, blissfully unaware
of how small their lives were about to become.

These Bodies

I dream I am barren.
I dream I sew myself shut.
If only I could reverse, reinvent us

as strangers, holding hands
at the window's ledge. The building burns
behind us. My skirt balloons on the downfall;
your tie draws up like a noose.

I don't pray. Instead, I close my eyes
and blackbirds appear, red cut
across their wings. This isn't the end
of our story. These bodies, falling,
don't even come close.

In Gratitude

Thank you to my posse of poem fixers, proofreaders and poetry workshop pals who helped me bring these poems into being. They include Marilyn Annucci, Carolyn Dale, Gwen Ebert, Barbara Edelman, Steve Hughes, Ellen Kreger Stark, Ellen McGrath Smith, Carroll Ann Susco, Kellie Wells, and the late Lucia Perillo. Much appreciation goes to my dear friend, the talented artist and graphic designer Rowan Moore-Seifred, who created this book's cover.

I am forever grateful to the University of Pittsburgh MFA program in creative writing for the guidance and support I received, especially from professors Toi Derricotte, Lynn Emanuel, Catherine Gammon and Ed Ochester. At Eastern Michigan University, where I earned my bachelor's degree, I was fortunate to have studied with Janet Kauffman who not only helped shape the writer I was to become, but who modeled being the teacher I strive to emulate. I am thankful to both institutions for introducing me to a lifelong community of talented writers with whom I continue to correspond and without whom many of these poems would not have seen the light of day. I am especially indebted to journalist and creative nonfiction writer Stephen S. Howie, my husband, to whom I dedicate this book.

Maria McLeod, 2022

Maria McLeod is a writer of poetry, prose and works of documentary theatre. She has worked as an interviewer, professor, journalist, PR consultant, ghost writer and oral historian in addition to mucking stalls, bartending, waiting tables, and whatever else she could do to keep herself afloat. In addition to publishing poetry and short stories, McLeod has authored works of documentary theatre based on interviews she's conducted, including *Body Talk: Sexual Triumphs, Trials, and Revelations*, a performance of monologues staged in Bellingham, Washington, and *First Person: Diverse Students Stories*, created for Western Washington University and performed on campus by WWU students. She also has collaborated on works of theatre dance, including a performance about prisons for a UNESCO conference on Prisons, Peace and Compassion. When she was a graduate student, earning an MFA in poetry at the University of Pittsburgh, she sometimes made appearances as a performance poet, achieving short-lived acclaim as the Lollapalooza poetry slam winner at Pittsburgh's Star Lake Amphitheater. McLeod has been a featured poet as part of the following reading series and/ or at these venues: Public Pool, Hamtramck, Michigan; Poet as Art, Lucia Douglass Gallery, Bellingham, Washington; Pittsburgh City Theatre; the Ceres Gallery, New York City; and the Andy Warhol Museum, Pittsburgh. Her work has been published in literary journals in the U.S., England and Scotland. Awards have included the *Indiana Review* Poetry Prize, judged by Denise Duhamel, and the Robert J. DeMott Short Prose Prize, judged by Thisbe Nissen. Her first chapbook, *Mother Want*, was named winner of the 2020 WaterSedge Poetry Chapbook Contest judged by Kim Stafford, Poet Laurette of Oregon 2018-20. Originally from the Detroit area, McLeod lives with her husband, writer Stephen S. Howie, in a cedar-shingled cabin surrounded by Western Red Cedars and Douglas Firs in the foothills of the North Cascades just south of Bellingham, Washington. She teaches writing and media studies as an associate professor of journalism for Western Washington University.

www.ingramcontent.com/pod-product-compliance
Lightning Source LLC
LaVergne TN
LVHW041517070426
835507LV00012B/1630